35 Ready-To-Go Ways to Publish Students' Research and Writing

By Michael Gravois

MARWICK

SCHOLASTIC
PROFESSIONAL BOOKS

New York • Toronto • London • Auckland • Sydney

Acknowledgments

To Jean Rubenstein, Rebekah Elmore, and
Andy Perry—mentors, masters, and friends

Cover design by Yuka Iwakoshi
Interior design by Sydney Wright

ISBN 0-590-05014-1

Copyright © 1998 by Michael Gravois
Printed in the U.S.A.

Contents

Introduction

If you give students each a piece of paper and ask them to write a report, you're often met with groans and complaints. But give these same students a piece of paper that has been folded into a circle book or cut into a data disk, and they readily start working. As every teacher knows, students quickly become bored with what they perceive as routine, so it is up to us to present information in interesting ways to keep students focused on the task at hand. Varying the activities not only makes schoolwork more stimulating, but makes each project stand out in the student's mind by giving him or her a unique visual reference, making it easier to remember the information.

The ideas presented in this book are based on the philosophy that learning should be a hands-on experience, and many of the activities require students to draw upon all of the language arts— reading, writing, speaking, and listening—as well as their art and design skills. To make this book even more helpful, each section describes how to create the various reporting formats and offer suggestions on how to use the ideas in your classroom. Many of the sections feature ready-to-go templates so the idea can be used immediately. And most of the ideas can be easily adapted to all the curriculum areas.

I hope you enjoy exploring the many reporting techniques described here and that your students find them as exciting and rewarding as mine do.

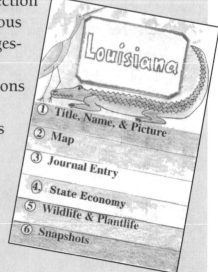

Lock Books

Lock books are indispensable teaching tools because they can be made quickly and additional pages can be easily inserted when needed. You can also adapt the size of a lock book to meet your needs. Instructions for creating lock books can be found on page 6.

How to Use Lock Books

❋ *Using the Template:* Students can use the templates on pages 7 and 8 to write a mini-autobiography. Make two-sided copies using both pages. The cover panel should be opposite panel 2. Students can cut out and assemble the books. This template creates an eight-page lock book measuring 4 1/4-by-5 1/2-inches.

❋ *Pre-design Lock Books:* When planning a lock book project, you can create a template for students to follow. First, construct a blank prototype and write your instructions on each page. Then unfold it, lay the pages side by side, and copy them. When students are ready to work on their lock books, the requirements will be preprinted on each page.

❋ *Experiment with Lock Books:* The instructions on the following pages are based on using 8 1/2-by-11-inch sheets of paper. However, you can use full or oversize sheets of paper to create bigger lock books. Experiment with different sizes and shapes of paper.

❋ *The Cover:* Each student should write his or her name and the title on the cover of the lock book (for example, "Angie's Lock Book of Laura Ingalls Wilder"). They should draw pictures on the cover related to their topic.

❋ *Homework, Classwork & Fieldtrips:* Lock books lend themselves to all subject areas. They can be used for recording homework and class assignments in math, science, social studies, and more. Students can also take lock books along with them on field trips to record things they see and learn, keeping them focused during the trip.

Name _____

Creating a Lock Book

Follow the directions below to create a lock book.

1. Cut a sheet of paper in half horizontally.

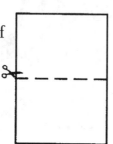

2. Fold both pieces of paper in half again.

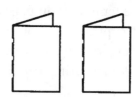

3. Open both pieces of paper. Measure along the crease and make two small pencil marks 1¹/2 inches and 4 inches from the top.

4. On one piece of paper, cut along the crease from the 1¹/2 inch mark to the 4 inch mark. (It may be helpful to first fold the paper in half lengthwise, but be careful not to crease it.)

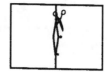

5. On the second piece of paper, cut along the crease from the top of the page to the 1¹/2 inch mark. Then cut along the crease from the bottom of the page to the 4 inch mark.

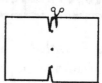

6. Take the piece of paper that has been cut at the top and bottom of the crease, fold one side of the paper, and feed it through the hole in the other page. (Be careful not to crease the page.) Unfold the page so it locks into place.

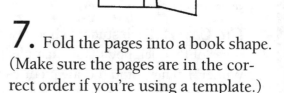

7. Fold the pages into a book shape. (Make sure the pages are in the correct order if you're using a template.)

8. Increase the book's length by feeding additional pages through the page with the hole in the center.

35 Ready-To-Go Ways to Publish Students' Research and Writing
Scholastic Professional Books

Clues

Across:

1. _____
_____
2. _____
_____
3. _____
_____
4. _____
_____

Down:

1. _____
_____
2. _____
_____
3. _____
_____
4. _____
_____

Page 6

Cover

Constructing the Lock Book

1. Cut the page in half along the dotted line.

2. Cut along the other dashed lines.

3. Feed the other page through the hole in this page. Make sure page three follows page two. Open it up so it locks into place.

4. Fold into a book shape.

5. Write your name on the cover.

Designing the Cover

✳ Draw self-portrait on the front cover. Write your name on the banner underneath the circle.

Back Cover

Draw a picture of something you like to do.
Fill the entire space with color and detail.

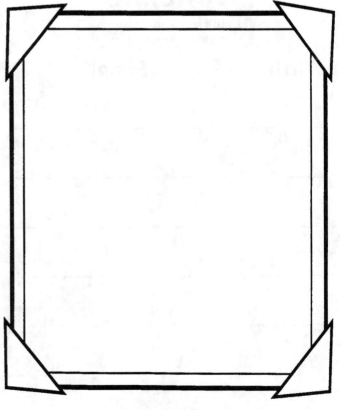

Page 3

All About Me

Write a complete paragraph about yourself.

_____

_____

_____

_____

_____

_____

_____

_____

_____

_____

Important Stats

Birthday: _____

Age: _____

Hair Color: _____

Eye Color: _____

Height: _____

Favorite Food: _____

Timeline

List five big events in your life
in chronological order.

Date   **Event**

_____   _____

_____   _____

_____   _____

_____   _____

Crossword Puzzle

Create a crossword puzzle based on things related to you.
You can use descriptive adjectives, your hobbies, or
favorite things as clues. Blacken in the unused spaces.
Write the clues on page 6.

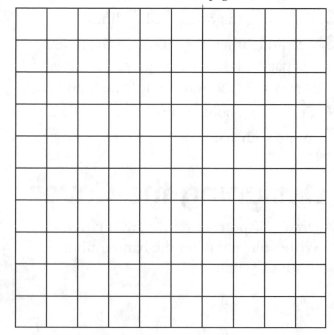

Little Books

Little books are easy to make and can be used for many different types of reports. The size and shape of the finished little book is determined by the size of the paper used, but an 8 1/2-by-11-inch piece of paper is perfect for most activities. See page 10 for complete instructions on making little books.

Creating a Little Book

※ **Predesign the Little Books:** Before assigning a little book, create a model book for students. Write the directions you want students to follow at the top of each panel. Make copies of the model and pass out to students. When students fold the paper into little books, each page will detail what they need to do.

※ **The Cover:** The cover should include the title and the student's name (for example, "Virginia's Little Book of Plate Tectonics"). It should also include a picture related to the topic.

※ **Filling Little Books:** Students can use their little books to record all kinds of information on a topic, including listing facts and figures, drawing graphs, illustrating ideas, writing summaries of research, completing graphic organizers, and creating timelines. You can tap into the multiple intelligences by requiring students to draw several pictures in their little books.

How to Use Little Books

※ **Homework and Class Work:** Little books are a great way for students to improve note-taking skills because just enough information can fit into a little book. Students are forced to identify the main ideas for the topic they are researching and record the information in a limited amount of space.

※ **Interactive Bulletin Boards:** Little books provide an attractive, easy-to-construct display for any topic the class is studying. Simply staple or tack the last page to the bulletin board. Students can learn more about a topic by flipping through their classmates' books.

Creating a Little Book

Follow the directions below to create a little book.

1. Fold a sheet of paper in half horizontally

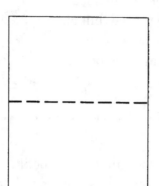

2. Fold it in half again in the same direction.

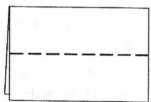

3. Fold this long narrow strip in half in the opposite direction.

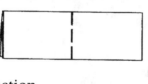

4. Open the paper up to the Step 2 position. Cut halfway down the vertical fold.

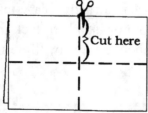

Cut here

5. Open the paper up and turn it horizontally. There will be a slit in the center of the paper where you've made the cut.

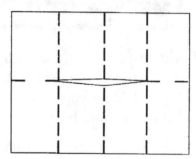

6. Fold the paper in half lengthwise.

7. Push in the ends of the paper until the center panels meet.

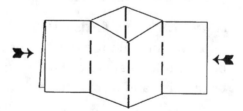

8. Fold the four pages into a book and crease the edge.

35 Ready-To-Go Ways to Publish Students' Research and Writing
Scholastic Professional Books

Advanced Techniques for Little Books

A little book has six single panels (seven including the back cover) or three double panels. However, you can create even more space with Hidden Panels and Secret Doors.

✳ *Hidden Panels:* Hidden panels are an effective way to add more information about a topic to a page. Record information behind the panels.

Version 1

• Create a lift-up panel by cutting the left and right hand seams of a page halfway up the sides. Glue the back of the top panel to the page behind it.

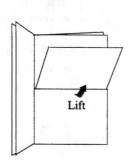

Version 2

• Create a panel that opens sideways by cutting halfway up the center seam of a double-page spread, and then horizontally across the page. (This technique only works on panels that have a connected seam on the outer edge.) Glue the back of the top panel to the page behind it.

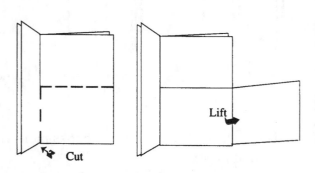

✳ *Secret Doors:* Secrets Doors are great for questions and answers or before and after illustrations.

• Draw the outline of a door in the center of a page. Cut out three sides of the door, leaving the fourth side to act as the hinge. Glue the perimeter of this panel to the page behind it.

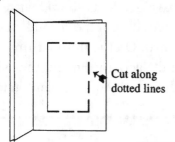
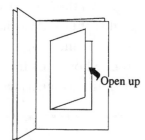

35 Ready-To-Go Ways to Publish Students' Research and Writing
Scholastic Professional Books

Circle Books

Circle books are easy to construct, fit a wide variety of uses, and make an attractive, colorful display hanging in the classroom. You can use any symmetrical shape, such as squares, triangles, stars, hearts, suns, or flowers, to create a circle book.

Creating a Circle Book

* **Using the Template:** Circle books can be any length, but four pages works for most projects. Start by making copies of the templates on pages 14 and 15. Each student will need four circle templates. To construct a circle book, have students follow the steps below:

 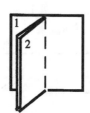  

1. Following the dotted lines, cut out each circle. Fold each circle in half.

2. Glue the back of side one to side two.

3. Glue side two to side three and side three to side four, and so on.

4. Complete the circle book by gluing the last side to side one.

* **Add Color:** Make the circle books more vibrant by copying the templates on colored paper.

How to Use Circle Books

* **Do/Feel/Learn:** One effective way for students to report information in a circle book is to use the do/feel/learn format. Pass out three writing pages and one drawing page. On the first writing page, students should write a paragraph describing what they did during an activity. On the second writing page, students should describe something they learned. On the third writing page, students should describe how they felt about the activity. Finally, they should draw a picture illustrating some aspect of the activity on the blank template.

✳ **Use Relevant Shapes:** Encourage students to tailor the shape of their circle books to their subject. For example, they can use stars, suns, and planets to report on space; flowers to report on plant life; triangles to illustrate mathematical rules such as the Pythagorean theorem or the area of a triangle; clouds to describe the different cloud formations; and hearts to describe the circulatory system.

Circle Book Projects

✳ **Mobiles:** For more complex projects and reports, have students complete several circle books to cover the topic. Each circle book can be a different shape and detail different aspects of a related topic. The completed shapes can be arranged in a mobile (perhaps hung from the bottom of a wire hanger) and then hung from the ceiling of the classroom.

✳ **Longer Circle Books:** Students can create circle books with as many as two dozen pages. Instead of gluing the last page to the first page, they can make a cover by gluing the first and last page to a sheet of poster board. (Secure the cover by squirting glue into the binding and setting it aside to dry.) You can display these by tacking the front and back covers to a bulletin board, allowing the pages to fan out. This is particularly effective when reporting on ecology or world history because the circular pages look like globes when they're attached to a bulletin board.

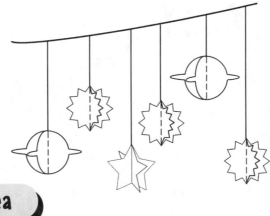

Display Idea

✳ **Circle Book Mobile:** Hang a string across your classroom. Tie varying lengths of thread from the string. Tie a paper clip to the end of each piece of thread and hang the circle book from the paper clip. When a breeze blows past the circle books, they spin and create a vibrant display to jazz up the classroom!

Circle Book Picture Template

✹ Use this shape for pictures.
✹ Be detailed, colorful, and creative. Fill the entire shape with color.
✹ Write your name at the bottom of this shape.

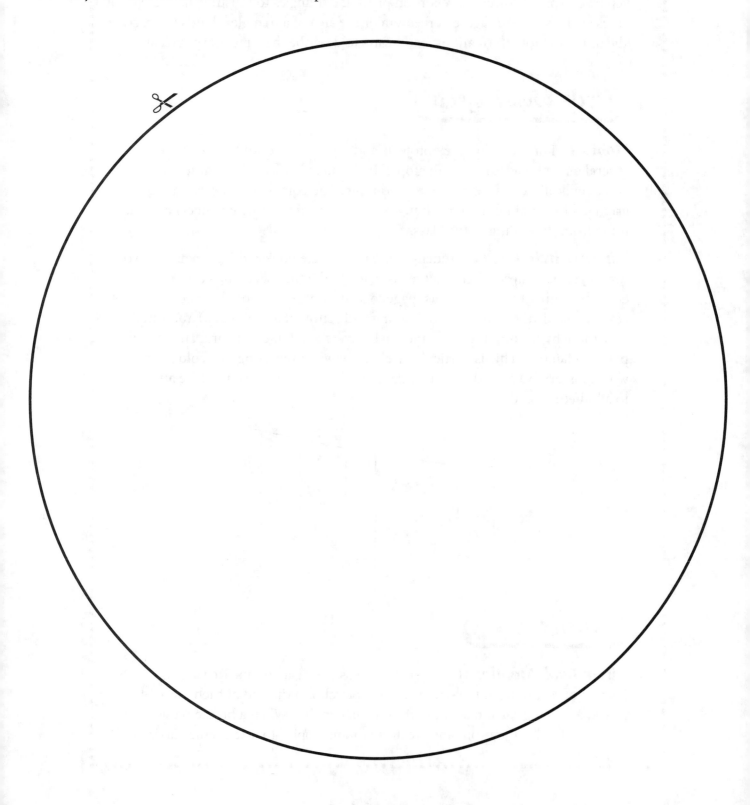

Circle Book Writing Template   Name _____

* Use this shape when writing paragraphs.
* Write neatly and use proper grammar, spelling, and punctuation.

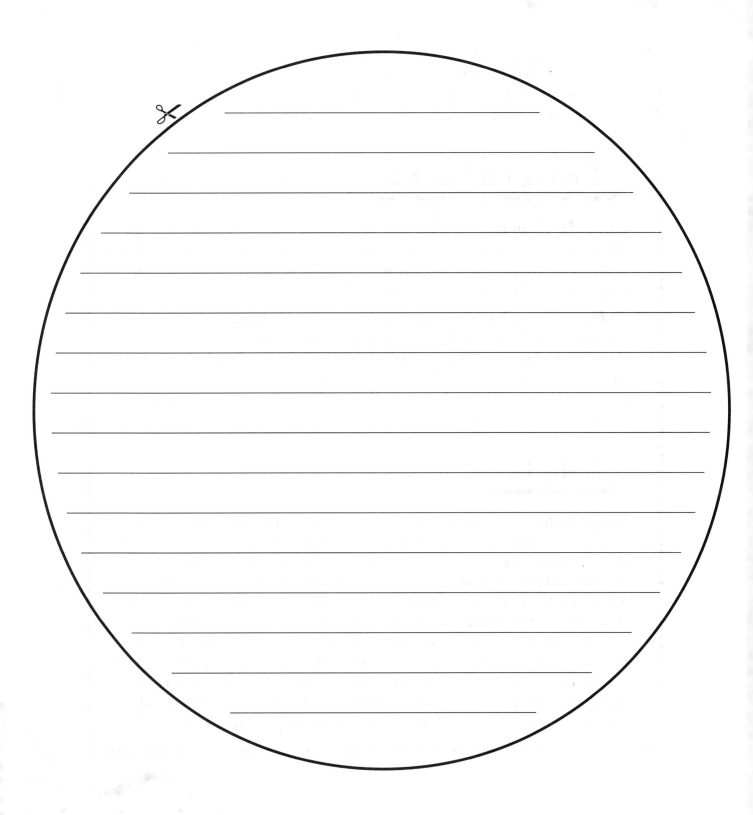

Name_____

B I N G O !

1	6	11	16	21
2	7	12	17	22
3	8	13	18	23
4	9	14	19	24
5	10	15	20	25

Instructions

* Find an answer that fits each of the questions above.
* Use the fact sheet to enter the information.
* Draw a thumbnail sketch in the square next to the fact.
* Draw an X over the space in the bingo board above.
* After answering all the categories in a row or column, put a √ in the circle.

Circle Book Writing Template   Name _____

* Use this shape when writing paragraphs.
* Write neatly and use proper grammar, spelling, and punctuation.

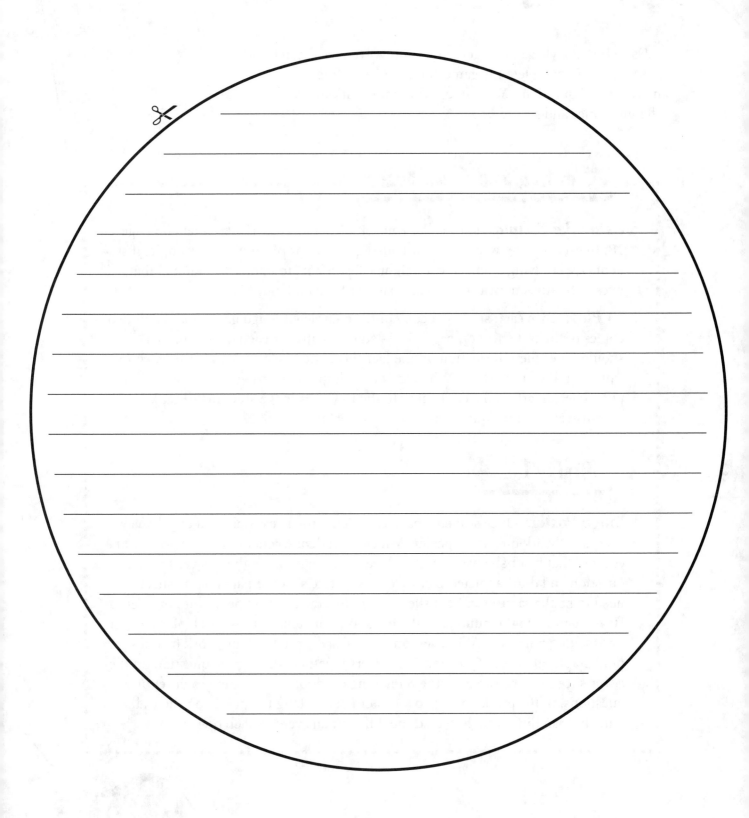

Bingo Research Game

Use a bingo-style game to get students involved in researching information. To complete the game, students must find the answers to 25 questions. You can use this game with many different topics and subjects.

Creating the Game Board

✳ ***Using the Template:*** To make your bingo game, copy the template on page 18. In each square, write an open-ended question or prompt. For example, if students are studying animals, you might ask students to name: "An animal that lives in South America" or "An animal that lives underground."

✳ ***To Play:*** Give each student a copy of the completed bingo game board and two copies of the fact sheet on page 17. As students answer each question, they should enter the information on the fact sheet and place an X over the category square on the bingo sheet. When they have found five answers in a row, they can put a check mark in the circle next to the row. Challenge students to see who can answer the most questions.

Display Idea

✳ ***Bingo Poster:*** Once students have completed their research, you can display everyone's work on a large poster. Ask each student to choose one bingo row or column that he or she has completed. Have students write the answer to each question and draw a related picture on a separate sheet of paper. (The sheets need to be the same size. I cut sheets of white construction paper into quarters.) Have them write the number of the question it matches on the back of the paper for tracking purposes. After everyone is finished, sort students' work by question. Staple all of the "Question 1" answers together, writing the question on the cover sheet. Do the same for the remaining questions. Next, glue each set of questions, in the proper order, to a poster board. Hang the poster on the wall. Students can flip through to read the different answers to each question.

Bingo Fact Sheet

Name_____

For each of the questions, write the answer and an interesting fact. Draw a thumbnail sketch in the square.

Question _____
1. Answer: _____
2. Interesting Fact: _____
_____
_____

Question _____
1. Answer: _____
2. Interesting Fact: _____
_____
_____

Question _____
1. Answer: _____
2. Interesting Fact: _____
_____
_____

Question _____
1. Answer: _____
2. Interesting Fact: _____
_____
_____

Question _____
1. Answer: _____
2. Interesting Fact: _____
_____
_____

Question _____
1. Answer: _____
2. Interesting Fact: _____
_____
_____

Question _____
1. Answer _____
2. Interesting Fact: _____
_____
_____

Question _____
1. Answer _____
2. Interesting Fact: _____
_____
_____

Question _____
1. Answer _____
2. Interesting Fact: _____
_____
_____

Question _____
1. Answer _____
2. Interesting Fact: _____
_____
_____

Name_____

B I N G O !

1	6	11	16	21
2	7	12	17	22
3	8	13	18	23
4	9	14	19	24
5	10	15	20	25

Instructions

* Find an answer that fits each of the questions above.
* Use the fact sheet to enter the information.
* Draw a thumbnail sketch in the square next to the fact.
* Draw an X over the space in the bingo board above.
* After answering all the categories in a row or column, put a √ in the circle.

Playbills

Students are often exposed to theater, whether its through reading plays, performing them in class, or seeing them as part of a field trip or assembly. Having students create playbills is a wonderful way for them to respond to a play they have seen or read. Review the requirements of this assignment before reading or viewing the play so students will know what elements they'll need to report on.

Creating a Playbill

✱ *Using the Template:* To create the playbill, make double-sided copies of the templates on pages 20 and 21 and then fold in half. If you create your own template for this project, try to include all of the elements that go into the dramatic experience: characters, costuming, sets, plot, protagonist/antagonist, problem/solution, lighting, the play's genre, playbill's cover design, etc.

✱ *Designing the Cover and Inside Pages:* On the cover students should write their last names and the word theater (for example, Dooley Theater). This way you'll know who designed each playbill. Students should design a cover that includes the title of the play, the playwright's name, and an illustration or logo that is representative of the play. To complete the rest of the playbill, students should follow the prompts on each page.

Display Idea

✱ *Bulletin Board:* Turn a bulletin board into a stage to display students' playbills. Create theater curtains out of bulletin-board paper. Give them a 3-D effect by bunching up the paper. Use a strip of corrugated border across the top to continue the curtain effect. In the center of the bulletin board, add a quote from the play or the famous quotation from the play *As You Like It*; "All the world's a stage..." Arrange the playbills around the quotation.

Draw a paper-doll figure of one of the characters in the play.
Create paper-doll clothes of the costumes he or she wore.
Include hats, purses, canes, or other props the character used.

Draw a detailed picture of the play's set.

Write the name of your favorite character in the circle. Brainstorm a list of words which describe this person. Write them on each line.

Write a two paragraph summary of the play's plot. Be sure to describe the main problem and solution.

Banners

When working on an important unit in school, creating banners provides a wonderful opportunity for the students to reflect on all that they have learned about a topic or subject.

Cc
Caring Counselors
by —
Maggie Reynolds

Creating the Banners

❋ **Advance Preparation:** Before beginning this activity, cut 13 strips of bulletin-board paper into 5-foot lengths. Turn each strip into two banners by cutting a V-shaped line across the middle of the paper. (See illustration below.) For variety, use several colors of bulletin-board paper.

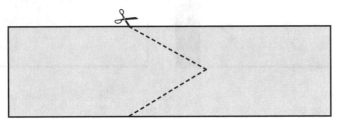

How to Use Banners

❋ **Brainstorming:** Write the letters A to Z down the left side of a large piece of chart paper. As a class, brainstorm all of the things related to the unit or topic that begin with each letter. Then choose one item from each letter that best represents the topic.

❋ **Illustrating:** Ask each student to select a different item and illustrate the idea on a square piece of white construction paper. Then students should glue their pictures to a banner and write a descriptive sentence or phrase under the picture. Hang the banners around the classroom.

❋ **Short Presentations:** Have each student write a short speech about his or her banner. Tell students to memorize their speeches and invite parents to hear the presentations. Parents will love to hear students share their work, while at the same time students will be practicing an important skill—public speaking! Leave the banners up for the rest of the term. You'll be amazed by how often they're referred to throughout the year.

Class Murals

Class murals are a fun way to get everyone involved in researching a topic and quickly designing and decorating a large area. Whether you're studying sea life, farm life, outer space, or Africa, murals provide a wonderful opportunity for students to become exposed to a broad range of information.

Creating a Class Mural

* **Design a Background:** Start by cutting a sheet of white bulletin-board paper to mural size. (I use a sheet of paper that is the length of the wall outside my classroom.) Lay the paper on the floor and have students create a background related to the unit you are studying (for example, the ocean bottom, a planet's surface, a savanna in Africa, etc.). You can assign small sections to each student so that everyone has his own space. You might even consider working with the art teacher on this phase of the project.

* **Brainstorm Topics:** After the background is drawn, have students brainstorm a list of things that are related to the topic you are studying. If the topic is oceans, your list might include seahorses, parrot fish, starfish, eels, urchins, and jellyfish. Each student picks a different item from the list, researches it, and draws a picture of it. (Consider allowing no more than two students to pick the same item. This will provide more visual variety in the mural.)

* **Research and Illustrate:** Students can use articles, books, and encyclopedias to research their subject. After completing their research, have students draw a picture of the item they have studied. (The size of the picture should be determined by its placement in the mural.) To make the mural three-dimensional, students can add extra elements to their illustrations. For example, fish with fins that stick out, comets with crepe-paper tails, and lions with manes made out of folded paper. On an index card, students should write a paragraph that includes four or five key facts they have discovered.

* **Report** Ask each student to give a short oral report on their findings and then attach the object and index card to the mural. Hang the mural in the hall or across a wall in the classroom.

Pop-up Books

Pop-up books are a fun, hands-on way for your students to tap into their higher-level thinking skills. Not only do students have to illustrate an idea, they have to illustrate the idea in a three-dimensional way.

Creating Pop-up Books

❋ **Modeling and Making Pop-ups:** Demonstrate the process of creating a pop-up page before asking students to make their own. Pass out copies of "Make Your Own Pop-up Book" on page 25 for students to refer to when they make their pop-up books.

How to Use Pop-up Books

❋ **Book Reports:** A five-page pop-up book is a great way for students to respond to literature. Ask students to use pop-up pages to respond to the different elements of a story such as plot, characters, setting, and conflict.

❋ **Class Pop-up Books:** To wrap up a theme unit or share the highlights of a field trip, create a class pop-up book. Have each student create a pop-up page of something they learned during the unit or on the field trip. Glue all of the pages together into one book, make a cover for it, and keep it in your classroom library.

❋ **Classwork:** If you ever need to work with small groups of students, pop-up books provide a focused, stimulating activity for the rest of the class to work on while you are busy with a small group. As you rotate between the small groups, everyone will have an equal opportunity to work on his or her pop-up book.

Make Your Own Pop-up Book

Follow the directions below to create a pop-up book.

1. Draw a rough sketch of the scene you wish to illustrate, and decide which elements will "pop up."

2. Fold a piece of construction paper in half horizontally. (An 8 1/2-by-14 -inch sheet will allow more writing space.)

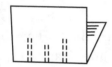

3. To create each pop-up tab, cut two slits along the folded edge. Varying the lengths of the tabs will make the scene more three-dimensional.

4. Open the paper up, and gently pull each of the pop-up tabs forward.

5. Fold the paper again so that each of the pop-up tabs falls into the center. Make a crease at the base of each tab.

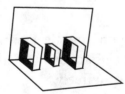

6. Open the paper up and illustrate the background.

7. On a separate sheet of paper, draw the pop-up elements of your scene. Cut the elements out and glue them to the front of a tab.

8. Use a ruler and pencil to lightly draw guidelines on the paper in front of your pop-up scene. Write a paragraph describing the scene.

9. Bind your book together by gluing the bottom of one page to the top of the next, until all of the pages are joined. Use a glue stick instead of glue so that the paper doesn't buckle. Be careful not to put glue where a tab on the opposite page will be or it will glue the tab closed and the page will rip.

10. Make a cover for your book by wrapping a large sheet of construction paper over pop-up pages. Glue it into place. Add a title and a cover illustration.

35 Ready-To-Go Ways to Publish Students' Research and Writing
Scholastic Professional Books

Super Trioramas

Students can report on all angles of a topic with super trioramas. Because there are four sides, super trioramas lend themselves to large projects. Students can use a super triorama at the end of a long research project or cooperative groups can work together on a super triorama. Directions for making super trioramas are on page 27.

How to Use Super Trioramas

✳ **Cross-Curricular Learning Tools:** A triorama can be used in all subject areas. For instance, if you were to use it in an ecology unit, each group could report on a type of pollution. The four sides of the "ecology pyramid" could cover the types of pollution, the causes of the pollution, the effects it has on the environment, and solutions to this problem. Other topics include states, continents, Native Americans, the human body, or book reports.

✳ **Cooperative Group Tip:** When grading cooperative projects, you should make each student responsible for the entire finished product. They should each proofread all of the writing and check for proper grammar and spelling.

Display Ideas

✳ **Hanging:** Punch a hole in the top of the super triorama and tie a string through the hole. Run a string across the back of the classroom and hang the trioramas from the string. This allows the trioramas to spin freely.

✳ **Free Standing:** To stand the super trioramas on a shelf or counter, make a simple cardboard base. Cut a piece of cardboard into four strips that are the same height and width as the bottom flaps of the triorama. Tape the strips behind the flaps of the pyramids so they can't be seen.

Name _____

Creating a Triorama

Follow the directions below to complete a Super Triorama.

1. Fold the top left corner of a piece of 8½-by-14-inch piece of construction paper diagonally so that the top edge of the paper is flush with the right edge of the paper.
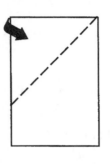

2. Fold the top right corner diagonally so that it touches the lower point of the previous fold.

3. Fold the panel at the bottom to make a horizontal crease along the edge.

4. Open the paper up and cut along the lower left diagonal crease to the center of the paper.

5. Pull point A over to point B so that the piece you cut is flush with the lower right diagonal crease. Glue the base into place.
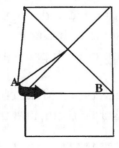

6. When four trioramas are finished, glue them together to form a pyramid. From underneath, tape the four lower panels so that they form four corners.
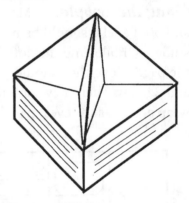

✱ **Designing the Inside:** Design the inside scenes of the triorama using any available craft materials—construction paper, string, fabric scraps, cotton, markers, and crayons—to make the scene three-dimensional. Write a brief paragraph describing the scene along the bottom flap. Make guidelines by lightly drawing pencil lines on the flap and then erasing the lines after writing the paragraph.

35 Ready-To-Go Ways to Publish Students' Research and Writing
Scholastic Professional Books

Flap Books

Flap books can help students tackle a big topic by breaking it into smaller elements. The state flap book template on the following pages is designed to be used during a unit on the 50 states. The prompts in the flap book help guide students' research.

① Title, Name, & Picture
② Map
③ Journal Entry
④ State Economy
⑤ Wildlife & Plantlife
⑥ Snapshots

Creating a Flap Book

✳ *Using the Template:* Make two-sided copies of the templates on pages 29 and 30. Panel 6 should be inverted on the back of panel 1. Pass out copies to students. Following the dotted lines, students should cut out the three panels on the page. Next, they should place the panels on top of each other, so panels 1, 2, and 3 show. Then they should bend the tops of the panels backward so they wrap around and reveal panels 4, 5, and 6. Fasten the top with two staples.

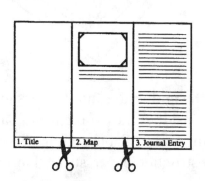

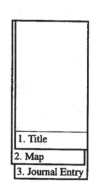

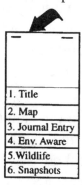

How to Use Flap Books

✳ *Making Your Own Flap Book Template:*
1. Determine the number of pages you want in your flap book, and then fold blank paper into a flap book of that length. Decide the size and length of the flap book by the amount of information you want the students to include.
2. Write the directions for each page on the top of each panel and add any other elements you want to include.
3. Open the book and lay the panels next to each other. Make copies of them. Students will only need to cut the panels out, fold, and staple them, and they're ready to go!

Draw a picture of the state bird and flower.
Write their names on the blanks.

STATE BIRD _____

STATE FLOWER _____

Draw a picture of a typical scene from this state.
Write a few sentences describing the scene.

_____
_____
_____
_____
_____
_____

3. State Snapshot

Write a few sentences describing
the state's major features.

_____
_____
_____
_____
_____
_____
_____
_____
_____
_____

Date Admitted to the Union:

_____

2. Map

1. Title, Name, and Picture

Draw a picture of a famous person associated with this state. Write his or her name in the banner.

Write a paragraph describing the achievements of the person.

4. Famous People

STATE FLAG

STATE NICKNAME

STATE MOTTO

5. State Symbols

Draw an outline of the state. Label the capital and major cities. Indicate the capital with a ★ and major cities with a •.

Write three interesting facts that you learned about the state. Use complete sentences.

1.

2.

3.

6. State Facts

Accordion Books

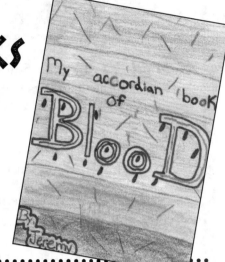

Accordion books are quick, easy-to-make response vehicles that can be used to report on an infinite number of subjects. They can be as short as 4 pages or as long as 16.

Creating an Accordion Book

✳ ***Using the Template:*** Students can use the template on page 33 to complete a biography on a famous person. Follow the directions below to construct an accordion book with the template.
   1. Make a copy of the page and cut the page in half along the dotted line.
   2. Tape the right edge of panel 4 to the left edge of panel 5. Tape the back of the panels so the tape does not cover the writing area.
   3. Accordion-fold the pages so that all of the writing is on the inside. (Panel 1 should be facing panel 2.) The top panel should be blank. Students can create their own cover for the book.

✳ ***Making Your Own Template:*** First, determine what information you want students to research and report. This will help you decide on the number of pages the accordion book should be. Then fold blank paper into an accordion book of that length. Write the directions for each page at the top of the panels. Open the book up, lay the panels next to each other, and make copies of the page. To complete the book, students only need to cut the panels out and fold them.

How to Use Accordion Books

✳ ***Timelines and Sequencing Activities:*** Because the panels of an accordion book are laid out in a left-to-right pattern, they lend themselves effectively to sequencing activities. Students can label the panels FIRST, NEXT, THEN, and FINALLY to describe the steps of a procedure; they can sequence events from a book they have read; they can create an "Accordion Book Autobiography" of their lives; or they can draw a timeline of a historical event.

✳ ***Making Patterns:*** Students can cut accordion books into different shapes. For example, students can use paper dolls for a book on the human body; cut a wave pattern across the top for a book on oceans; use a heart shape for a book on circulation or a report on *Romeo and Juliet*; or make a link of clouds for a study of weather patterns. Students can use their imaginations to come up with a pattern related to their topics.

✳ ***Sturdier Books:*** Students can make more durable accordion books by folding a rectangular sheet of butcher-block paper in half lengthwise and folding it into an accordion book. The two-ply pages will prevent markers from bleeding through and students will be able to design panels and doors in their books. Make the covers sturdier by gluing a piece of cardboard behind the front and back covers.

✳ ***Hidden Panels and Secret Doors:*** The same techniques used for creating additional panels and doors in little books (see page 11) can be used with accordion books. Students can experiment by cutting panels in different ways to vary the way information is presented.

Display Idea

✳ ***3-D Bulletin Board:*** Accordion books make an attractive display for any bulletin board. Staple the first and last pages to the bulletin board so that the inside pages can be seen. Keep some of the accordion effect so it looks three-dimensional.

List ten major events in this person's life.

Date   Event

4

List words you would use to describe this person.

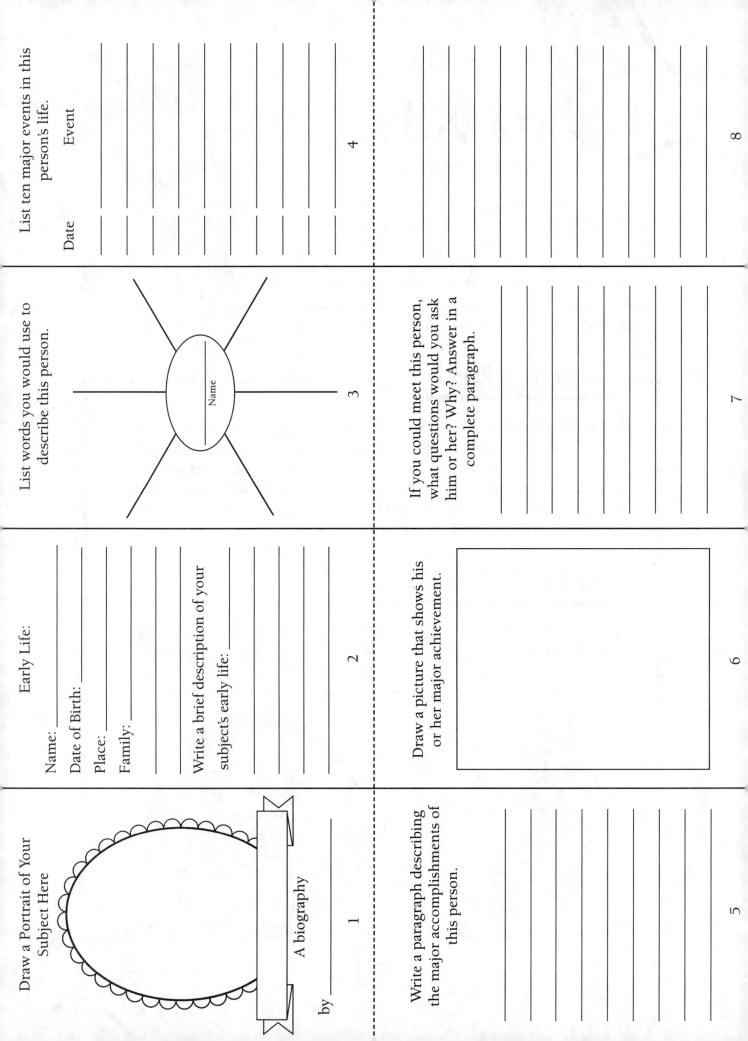

Name

3

Early Life:

Name: _____
Date of Birth: _____
Place: _____
Family: _____

Write a brief description of your subject's early life: _____

2

Draw a Portrait of Your Subject Here

A biography

by _____

1

8

If you could meet this person, what questions would you ask him or her? Why? Answer in a complete paragraph.

7

Draw a picture that shows his or her major achievement.

6

Write a paragraph describing the major accomplishments of this person.

5

Data Disks

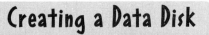

A data disk is an interactive way for students to report information and to read their classmates' research. Students can make a simple data disk by securing two circles together with a brass fastener. As they become more familiar with the format, they can design and produce more elaborate data disks. There are an infinite variety of styles, each one suited to a different purpose.

Creating a Data Disk

✳ ***Using the Template:*** The data disk template on page 35 is a great way to introduce students to the format. Students simply fill-in three questions and answers. To complete the disk, students should include their names and topics on the cover (i.e., "Karen's Data Disk of Roanoke Island") and add a picture or decorative border. Students can use this format to answer questions about a topic, share facts they have uncovered, or explain new terms.

How to Use Data Disks

✳ ***A Variety of Data Disk Styles:*** On this page there are three styles of data disks. The designs can be adapted to fit many needs. For example, in the "Data Disk of Digestion," the student explains four steps of digestion. "Carly's Data Disk of Roanoke Island" features questions and answers about the Roanoke Island.

Data Disk Template

Name _____

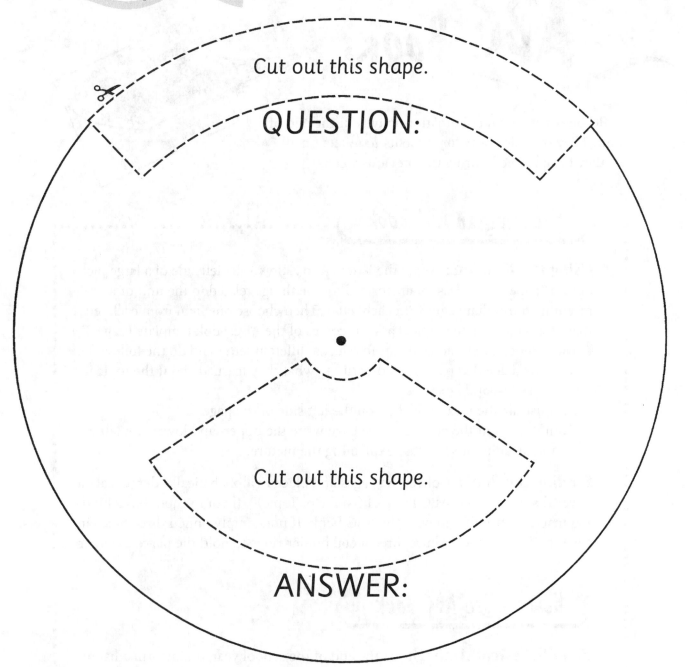

Cut out this shape.

QUESTION:

Cut out this shape.

ANSWER:

1. Glue the template onto a sheet of construction paper or poster board. Cut out the data disk but do not cut out the windows yet.

2. Using the data disk template, draw a second circle on oaktag or white construction paper and cut the circle out.

3. Cut out the windows on the data disk template.

4. Place the data disk on top of the second circle, and fasten together with a brass

fastener. Push the fastener through the black dot in the center of the data disk.

5. Write the first question in the question box and write the answer in the answer box. Rotate the data disk and fill in your second question and answer. Rotate the disk again and fill in your third question and answer.

6. Write the title "(Your Name)'s data disk of (Subject)" across the center of the data disk. Draw a related picture.

ABC Books

ABC books are a fun culminating activity at the end of a unit. They provide a way for students to reflect on all that they have learned during the previous weeks.

Creating an ABC Book

❋ **Using the Template:** Write the letters A to Z down the left side of a large piece of chart paper. As a class, brainstorm all of the things related to the unit or a recent field trip that begin with each letter. Then choose one item from each letter that best represents the topic. Pass out copies of the ABC book template (page 37) to each student. Ask each student to select a different letter and do the following:

1. Write a detailed paragraph describing what they learned about the topic in the right-hand box.
2. Illustrate the idea in the box on the left side of the page.
3. In the box at the bottom of the page write the upper- and lowercase letter and an alliterative phrase explaining the picture.

❋ **Binding the Book:** Collect the pages and place in alphabetical order. Create a cover that reads "Our ABC Book of (Name of Topic)". If your school has a binding machine, use that to bind the ABC book. If not, simply punch three holes in the top of each page and use three metal binder rings to hold the pages together.

How to Use ABC Books

❋ **End-of-the-Year Activity:** At the end of the school year, brainstorm a list of things that the class learned during the year and create an ABC book of 26 highlights. On the first day of the next school year, read the "ABC's of Fifth Grade" to your new class. It will get students excited about all the things they will do in the coming year.

❋ **Class Library:** After reviewing the ABC book with the class, add it to the class library so students can refer to it throughout the year.

ABC Book Template

In the box at the bottom of the page, write the upper- and lowercase letters you are illustrating, an alliterative phrase that describes the picture, and your name. Draw the picture on the left. Write a paragraph describing your illustration on the right.

Writing Cubes

Turn writing assignments into three-dimensional displays with writing cubes.

Creating a Writing Cube

* ***Using the Fable Cube Template:*** The template on pages 39 and 40 can be used during a unit on fables. The instructions for filling out and putting the cube together are on the template. With slight modifications, this cube can be used as a response vehicle for other genres as well.

* ***Creating a Template:*** You can create a blank cube template using the fable cube on pages 39 and 40. Either trace the outline of the cube on another sheet of paper or cover the text on the cube and then copy it. Create a requirement sheet that details six elements you want students to report on. One panel on the cube should include the student's name, the project title, and perhaps a small illustration. Hand out copies of the requirement sheet with the blank template.

Display Idea

* ***Hanging Cubes:*** Create a mobile of students' writing cubes. Hang a string across the classroom. Tie threads of varying lengths along the string. Tie a paper clip to the end of each piece of thread. Fasten the writing cubes to the thread with paper clips so they create a long mobile of students' work. This allows the viewer to see all six sides of the writing cubes.

Fable Cube Template

Name_____

1. Fill out each of the panels according to the instructions below.

     PANEL 1:   Using creative lettering, write the name of the fable,
                         the author of the fable, and your name.

     PANEL 2:   Write a brief summary of the fable.

     PANEL 3:   Write the moral of the fable.

     PANEL 4:   Use at least three complete sentences to explain the meaning of the moral.

     PANEL 5:   Draw a detailed picture of the fable.

     PANEL 6:   Fill out "Elements of a Story"

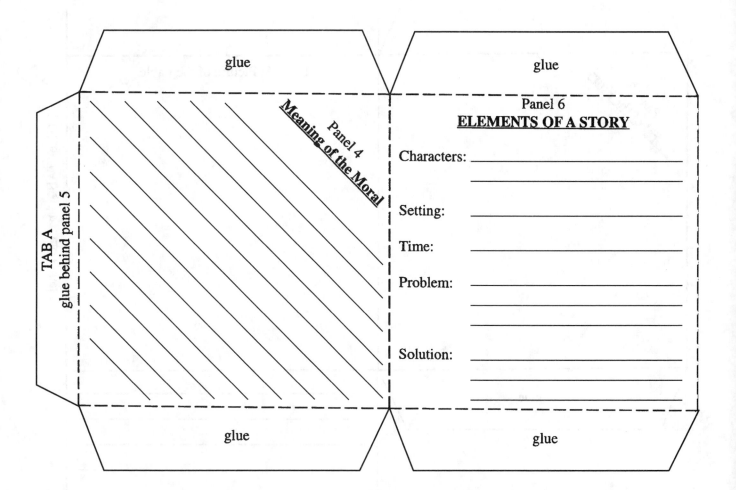

2. Cut out the cube pieces along the solid lines.

3. Glue tab A behind panel 5.

4. Fold along the dotted lines so it forms a cube.

5. Glue each of the tabs behind the panel they meet.

Fable Cube Template

Panel 1: Title, Author, and Name

glue

Panel 3
Moral of the Story

Panel 5: Picture of the Fable

Glue "TAB A" behind Panel 5

glue

_____
_____
_____
_____
_____
_____
_____
_____
_____
_____
_____
_____
_____

Panel 2
SUMMARY

Interactive Notebooks

Developing note-taking skills and learning to identify the main idea of written passages are important teaching objectives during the middle school years. Yet taking notes can seem like a grueling task to many students. Interactive notebooks can help students learn how to take notes by having them break information into digestible chunks and present it in a visually interesting, hands-on, and organized way.

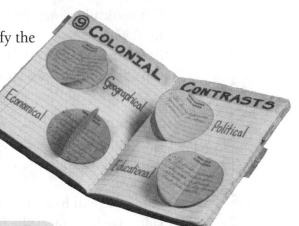

Creating an Interactive Notebook

✳ *Getting Started:* While interactive notebooks require creative planning on the teacher's part, the results are well worth the effort. To get started, consider adapting one or two activities from each unit into interactive-notebook form. Each year adapt a little more. Before you know it, you'll have full units using this approach.

✳ *Materials:* Each student will need a composition notebook to turn into an interactive notebook. (This type of notebook works best and the binding is easier to work with than a spiral notebook.)

Interactive Notebook Techniques

✳ *Question and Answer Strips:* Students can use these lift-the-flap strips to answer homework or textbook questions—and they are great way to review before a test. To make the strips:

1. Use a right-hand page. If there are five questions to be answered, cut six horizontal strips in the page. (One for the title strip.)
2. Glue the top strip to the page behind it and write the title of the exercise or activity on the strip.
3. Write a question on each of the strips and write the answer on the page directly behind the question strip.

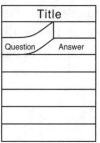

Hidden Panels: Students can use hidden panels to record information about a cause and an effect. To make a page with a flap at the bottom:

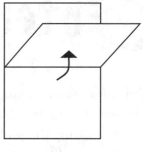

1. Cut vertically along the inside margin halfway up the page.
2. Fold the page up so the bottom edge meets the top edge, and make a crease.
3. Glue the top of the page to the page behind it.

Column Panels: Students can use this type of panel to compare and contrast information, sequence events, or add illustrations. To create a page with four column panels:

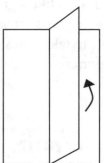

1. Fold a page in half vertically, bringing the outside edge in to meet the inside margin.
2. Glue the inside panel to the page behind it.

Double Page Spreads: Students can create two-page spreads in their notebooks if they have a lot of information related to one topic. To make two-page spreads:

1. Tape the side edges of two pages together. Cut along the margin of the top page. This allows the top page to fold out, revealing an interior double-page spread.

Pocket Pages: Student can add pockets to their notebooks to store supplementary materials such as letters, data disks, and little books. To make a pocket:

1. Cut a page in half horizontally. Remove the top part of the page by cutting along the inside margin. (Or just glue the top panel to the page behind it.)
2. Tape the side and bottom edges of the bottom panel to the page behind it.

Support Materials: Many of the other activities in this book can be adapted and used for classwork and homework assignments and then glued directly into an interactive notebook—including little books, accordion books, circle books, flap books, lock books, data disks, and travel guides.

Video Cameras

Video cameras document all facets of life today. But it wasn't too long ago that these machines didn't exist. What images would we have seen if Columbus had taken a video camera with him on his historic voyage? What wonders would be documented on a microscopic trip through the human body? With this reporting device and students' imaginations, we just might know!

Creating a Video Camera

* ***Using the Templates:*** Hand out copies of the templates on pages 46 and 47. Ask each student to create six illustrations, using the film strip template, to explain their subject. Next, they should write a descriptive paragraph, using the writing strips template, to accompany each illustration.

* ***Making the Camera:*** Hand out copies of the video camera templates on pages 44 and 45. Following the directions on the templates, students can cut out and assemble the video cameras. To make the frame sturdier, students can glue the templates to poster board or cardboard.

* ***Putting It All Together:*** Students cut out their writing strips, put them in order, and staple them to the video camera. Then students cut out the film frames and, following the directions on the template, thread the frames through the camera.

* ***Adding Panels:*** If students need more panels for art and illustration, make additional copies of the templates.

How to Use Video Cameras

* ***Report Ideas:*** Video cameras can be used for countless activities. Students can create a video biography of someone's life; take you on a journey through foreign countries; report on a field trip; or pretend a character in a book held a video camera throughout the story. Write a requirement sheet to let the students know what information is required, and let their imaginations take over.

Video Camera Cover

Name _____

1. Glue this to a sheet of poster board and cut it out.

2. Color the video camera.

3. Write your name and the title of your report in the square at the bottom of the video camera. Use creative lettering.

Video Camera Interior

Name _____

1. Glue this sheet to a sheet of poster board and cut it out.

Tape the cover template to this top line so it can be lifted up, revealing the interior of the video camera.

Place writing sheets here.

Put your writing sheets in order and staple the left edges so they cover these directions.

Slot A

Cut slots A and B. Thread your film through slot A from behind and down through slot B so only one frame can be seen at a time. Then tape each end tab around a craft stick to prevent it from being pulled through.

Slot B

Video Camera Film Strips

Name _____

After you thread your video tape through the camera, tape this tab to a craft stick or pencil.

After you thread your video tape through the camera, tape this tab to a craft stick or pencil.

Glue this tab behind panel 3.

Video Camera Writing Strips

Name _____

Panel #   :

Panel #   :

Panel #   :

Panel #   :

Scrapbooks

Scrapbooks are personal journals that intimately reflect the individual who created them. A student can conduct a meaningful character study by compiling a scrapbook as if he or she were another person. This project requires thoughtful attention to the details of what makes individuals unique.

Creating a Scrapbook

✳ **Binding the Scrapbook:** Give each student five large sheets of construction paper to use as the scrapbook. If you have a binding machine, you should bind the sheets of paper together along the short side. Otherwise, students can design a binding to hold the sheets together.

✳ **Using the Templates:** Pass out copies of the picture templates on page 49. Students should design photographs or illustrations that the scrapbook's "creator" might have taken. For example, the pictures can be scenes from a historical figure's life or scenes from a book character's life. Students should write a caption for each picture. They can also add any other elements that reflect the person.

How to Use Scrapbooks

✳ **Book Reports:** Have students create a scrapbook as if it were made by a character in a novel that they have read. It could include letters from other characters, souvenirs of significant events, diary entries, pictures of the settings and characters, and more.

✳ **Historical Figures:** Students can create a scrapbook for a famous person they are studying in class. For example, a pioneer traveling west in a covered wagon or a settler in Jamestown.

✳ **End-of-the-Year Scrapbooks:** Compile a class scrapbook of major events that happened throughout the year. Each student can design a page. This can be added to the classroom library for future classes to look through.

Scrapbook Template

Use these frames to draw pictures for your scrapbook. Fill the entire frame with color. Cut the pictures out and glue them into the scrapbook. Write a caption next to each picture.

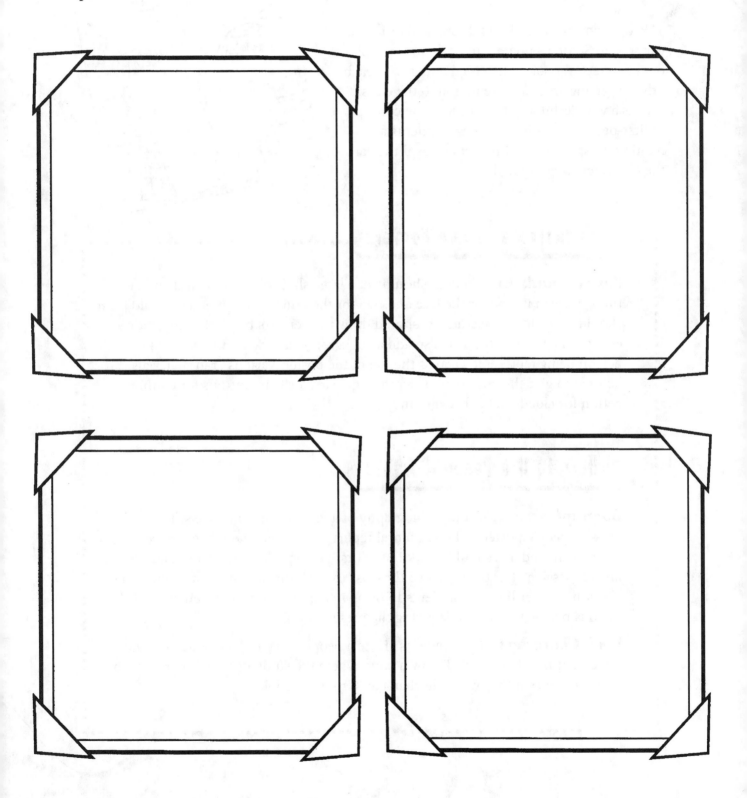

People Posters

John Paul Jones

People posters add a bit of dramatic flair to the classroom. Students pretend to be famous people or characters in books while interacting with each other or giving an oral presentation to the class. This is a wonderful way to introduce the concept of first-person narratives, because students are required to speak in the first person, as if they are the characters they studied.

Creating a People Poster

✹ **Poster Board:** Each student should get a large sheet of poster board and cut three holes in it: one for the face and two for the arms. The armholes should be at shoulder height. Then students should draw the person's body, clothing, hair, etc., on the board. They can also add a background and write the name of the person being represented across the top of the poster. Various craft materials can be used to give the poster some depth (e.g., yarn for hair, buttons for clothing, cotton for clouds in the background, etc.).

How to Use People Posters

✹ **Biographies:** After reading a biography of a famous person, have students create a people poster and give an oral report of that person's life while wearing the poster. Students should speak in the first person. Plan a question-and-answer session after the report so the class can ask the famous visitor questions about his or her life. Ask students to bring in a prop that is representative of the famous person to hold while giving the presentation.

✹ **Book Characters:** Have students create a people poster of a character in a novel that they have read. Throw a party where the students must interact with one another as if they were the characters from the book.

Internet Poster Requirement Sheet

Title:
- Write the title of the subject you researched across the top of the poster. List the names of each of your group members.

Graphic Organizer:
- As a group, brainstorm the list of the steps you took in order to: 1.) log on to the Internet, 2.) get to your search engine, 3.) find the information related to your topic. Include everything that needs to be typed, the number of clicks needed to open documents, the words you need to click on to access information.
- Create a graphic organizer that presents this information so someone who has never used the Internet will be able to find his or her way to your topic.
- Attach the graphic organizer to your poster.

Terminology Chart:
- As a group, define the following terms in your own words: **Internet, World Wide Web, URL, Web page, Hyperlink, Query box, Hit, Modem, Scroll bar, Query** (Explain what *and/or* do), **Search engine** (Mention some examples of search engines).
- Attach the terminology chart to your poster.

Search Engine Web Page:
- Print out a copy of a Web page or search engine page from the Internet.
- Highlight any of the words that are also on the terminology chart.
- Explain what each of these buttons do: Back, Forward, Reload, Search, Stop.
- Attach this page to your learning poster.

Safety Rules:
- Use the safety templates to describe the four rules for safety on the Internet.

Interesting Information:
- Read through the information you printed out from the topic you researched.
- Each person in the group should choose one interesting fact and write a detailed paragraph about it and then draw a picture to accompany the paragraph.
- Glue each paragraph and drawing to a sheet of construction paper and attach to the poster.

35 Ready-To-Go Ways to Publish Students' Research and Writing
Scholastic Professional Books

Safety Templates

- Use these templates to create the safety-rules icons.
- Draw an icon for each rule inside of the symbol. Make it colorful!
- Cut out each symbol and attach it to a piece of construction paper.
- Write the rule underneath the icon.
- Attach them to your poster

Travel Guides

Whether you're studying your own town or city, major cities of the world, the 50 states, the different regions of the United States, countries of the world, or the seven continents, creating travel guides helps students focus on the important characteristics of a region.

Creating a Travel Guide

✳ ***Using the Template:*** Make two-sided copies of the templates on pages 56 and 57. (Panel 3 should be on the back of panel 1.) Students can follow the directions on the back panel to complete their travel guides. For a more polished final product, copy the templates on sheets of heavier card-stock paper.

✳ ***For More Information:*** Teach your students how to write business letters by having them write to tourist bureaus requesting information about the area on which they are reporting. You can also visit a local AAA (American Automobile Association) office and ask if it would supply catalogs of the states your class is studying. These catalogs can become a part of your class reference library.

Display Idea

✳ ***Bulletin Board:*** Display travel guides by stapling the interior middle panel to a bulletin board. The left and right panels can then be opened by anyone interested in learning more about the region. Post a map of the area the class studied in the center of the bulletin board.

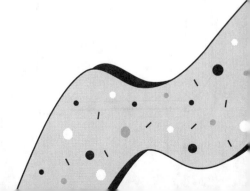

DIRECTIONS

Following the dashed lines, fold paper in thirds. Panel 1 will be the cover of your guide.

CREATING THE PANELS

PANEL 1: This will be the cover of your guide. Include a title, your name, and an illustration which is representative of the area. Be creative and detailed.

PANEL 2: Draw pictures of two attractions or sites that are in the area. Make sure the pictures fill the entire frame; do not leave white space. Write a complete, detailed sentence describing each picture.

PANEL 3: Write about the history of the area. Describe when it was founded, important events and people in its history, and other items of note.

PANEL 4: Top: Draw a map that gives an overview of the area. Note major points of interest. Include a key. Bottom: List the vital statistics of the area as indicated.

PANEL 5: Write a descriptive paragraph to entice the reader to visit the area. Create a headline for this section.

Back Cover

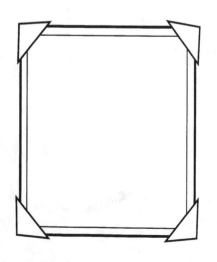

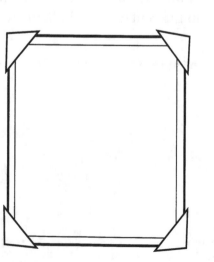

VITAL STATISTICS

Size: _____

Population: _____

Economic Sources: _____

_____

Climate: _____

Language Spoken: _____

Points of Interest: _____

_____

HISTORY

3.

4.

5.

Dictionaries

No matter what the grade level, increasing students' vocabulary is a goal of every teacher. Having students compile a personal dictionary is a great way for them to remember and review new words they learn during the year.

Creating a Dictionary

* **Personal Dictionaries:** Although setting up the dictionary takes a little bit of time, students can use it all year. Have students bring in a composition notebook, and then follow the steps below to create a dictionary with tabbed pages.
    1. On the first page of the notebook, draw a vertical line $1/2$ inch from the right side of the page.
    2. On the top line, to the right of the line you drew, write the letter A.
    3. Cut along the vertical line up to the letter A. Then cut horizontally across the line underneath the letter. Cut the next three pages in the same way.
    4. On the second line of the fourth page write the letter B.
    5. Cut this page and the next three up to the line underneath the letter "B".
    6. Continue doing this for each letter of the alphabet. (X Y and Z can be combined if there is not enough space for each letter.).

How to Use Dictionaries

* **Word of the Day:** Teach new vocabulary words by posting a WORD OF THE DAY in your classroom. Students can create an entry for the word in their dictionaries with the following information: the word and its part of speech; a definition; a synonym for the word; an antonym for the word; and a sentence using the word that explains what the word means.

    After students have completed their entries, review the word with the class and ask for volunteers to read their sentences aloud. Consider starting your language arts class with a word of the day; it's a great activity for students to work on at the beginning of class.

Maps & Travelogues

Draw students into the lives and experiences of journeymen, pioneers, and explorers with maps and travelogues. Plotting a journey on a map provides students with a visual reference of the places a traveler has visited. Writing a travelogue encourages students to imagine the journey from the traveler's perspective.

Creating a Map and Travelogue

✳ **Creating the Maps:** To make the maps and travelogues, students will need large sheets of white paper. Leaving a 2-inch margin at the top and bottom of the page, students should draw a map that traces their subjects' journeys. They should also highlight five places on the map where something significant happened, numbering the points from 1 to 5. The maps should be detailed and include a key. On the back, students should write a paragraph, from the traveler's perspective, describing each of the five points highlighted on the map. Finally, have students turn the map into a scroll by curling the top over and taping it to the back and curling the bottom under and taping it.

How to Use Maps and Travelogues

✳ **Historical Writing:** Students can read about famous explorers, plot maps of their journeys, and write travelogues from the explorers' points of view describing their accomplishments and setbacks. Students can report on the travels of immigrants to America or early pioneers on their journey west.

✳ **Creative Writing:** Many novels for young adults either center around a journey a character takes or describe an area where a character lived (e.g., *My Side of the Mountain*, *Island of the Blue Dolphin*, *Walk Two Moons*, *Hatchet*, and so on). Students can create maps that show the places featured in the story and write journal entries describing them.

✳ **Geographical Writing:** Students can create maps of cities, states, or countries; mark the locations of important sites; and write about the significance of each of the sites.

Quicksheets

Page 89

Charlotte hopes to save Wilbur's life by writing the word "TERRIFIC" in her web.

Quicksheets are like visual Cliff's Notes for novels you read in class. Quicksheets act as both a storyboard and book synopsis.

Creating a Quicksheet

* **Using the Templates:** Make copies of the quicksheet templates on page 61 and hand out to students. As you read a novel in class, assign one or more pages to each student. Students should reread their assigned page for homework, write the main idea from that page on the quicksheet, and draw a picture of the main idea in the box. They should also write the page number at the top of the quicksheet. Students can cut out the completed quicksheets and punch holes in the top of the page where indicated.

* **Spotlighting the Main Idea:** Students can use quick sheets to record the key points or main ideas of any independent reading assignments.

Display Idea

* **A String of Quicksheets:** For easy reference, hang quicksheets from a string. Place the quicksheets in order and weave a string through the holes. The quicksheets can be hung up as they are completed so that the students can have a quick reference of things that happened previously in the novel.

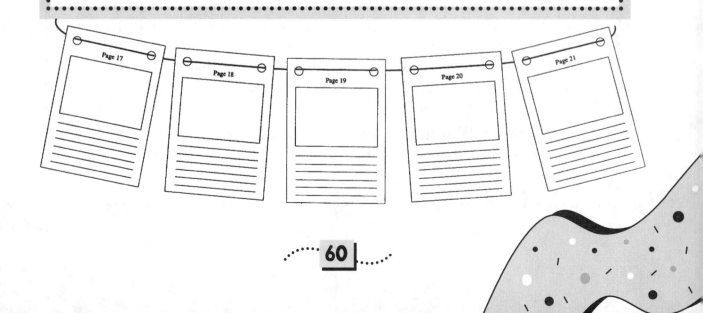

Quicksheet Templates

Name _____

◯   Page ___   ◯

◯   Page ___   ◯

◯   Page ___   ◯

◯   Page ___   ◯

Class Chronicles

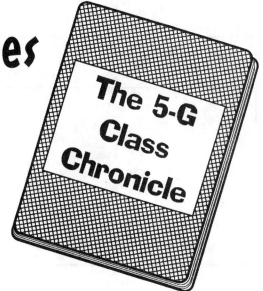

The 5-G Class Chronicle

Consistent home-and-school communication is an important factor in ensuring a successful school year. Yet with the many duties a teacher has to perform it is difficult to find the time to inform parents of school activities and upcoming events. Sharing this responsibility with students is a helpful way to both publish students' writing on a regular basis and inform parents what is happening in your classroom.

Creating a Class Chronicle

❋ **Nightly Reporting:** At the beginning of the school year, label a notebook THE CLASS CHRONICLE. Each night, select one student to be the day's reporter and send the chronicle home with him or her. (You can use a class list to check off names as each student takes it home to ensure that each child has a chance.) In the notebook, students should write a two- or three-paragraph article that describes something they did that day in school, something they learned, and how they felt about the day's activities. They should put the day's date and their name at the beginning of the article. The next day, students should type the article on the computer under a predesigned banner reading THE CLASS CHRONICLE.

❋ **Compiling the Chronicle:** At the end of the week you will have five typed articles. (If students don't have access to a computer, they can neatly rewrite the article.) Add a short paragraph that includes your thoughts about the week, information about upcoming events or thematic units, requests for parent volunteers, and other pertinent information. Print out the chronicle, copy it, and send it home with your students. Parents will appreciate the regular correspondence, and it will become a valuable tool to fuel at-home discussions about what has happened that week in school.

Jeopardy!

Students love to play games. Just think about the reaction you get when you tell them that you're going to have a spelling bee or social studies bee. This activity allows the students to research and review information while they create a game for the class.

FAMOUS QUOTES

He said, "Give me liberty or give me death!"

He said, "I regret that I have but one life to give for my country."

He said, "Don't fire until you see the whites of their eyes."

He said, "We must all hang together or we will all hang separately."

He said, "The British are coming! The British are coming!"

Creating the Jeopardy! Game Board

✳ ***Reviewing the Rules:*** The game show Jeopardy! is unique in that the answers and questions are revealed in reverse. Ask students to watch the game at home and then, as a class, create sample answers and questions so students can practice the format.

✳ ***Using the Templates:*** Pass out copies of the templates on page 64. Have students cut out the question strips and glue them to a piece of construction paper. (For ease and safety, you might want to use a razor blade to cut the four answer boxes out yourself and give a precut template to each student.) Students then write four questions and answers based a particular topic on the template. Following the Jeopardy! format, students should write the answers on the front of the flaps and the questions under the flaps.

✳ ***Putting It Together:*** Attach each student's game piece to the large sheet of bulletin-board paper, add a title that reflects the subject area, and hang the poster up. Play your own game of Jeopardy! using this gameboard. After the game is finished, students can use this display as a study guide.

How to Use Jeopardy!

✳ ***Culminating Activity:*** This is a great tool for reviewing everything that has been covered during a unit. As a class, brainstorm a list of possible categories and allow students to choose a category from the list.

✳ ***Cross-Curricular Study:*** Because of the open-ended nature of this game, it can be used in all curricular areas, from music and art to reading and science. You can also cover several curriculum areas in one game.

Jeopardy! Templates

Name _____

1. Cut the templates out. Following the solid lines, cut out the four answer boxes. Fold each flap along the dotted line.
2. Glue the template to a sheet of construction paper. Glue around each of the flaps. Do not glue the flaps.
3. Write the name of the category in the top box.
4. Write an answer in each of the four answer boxes. Lift the flaps and write the questions.

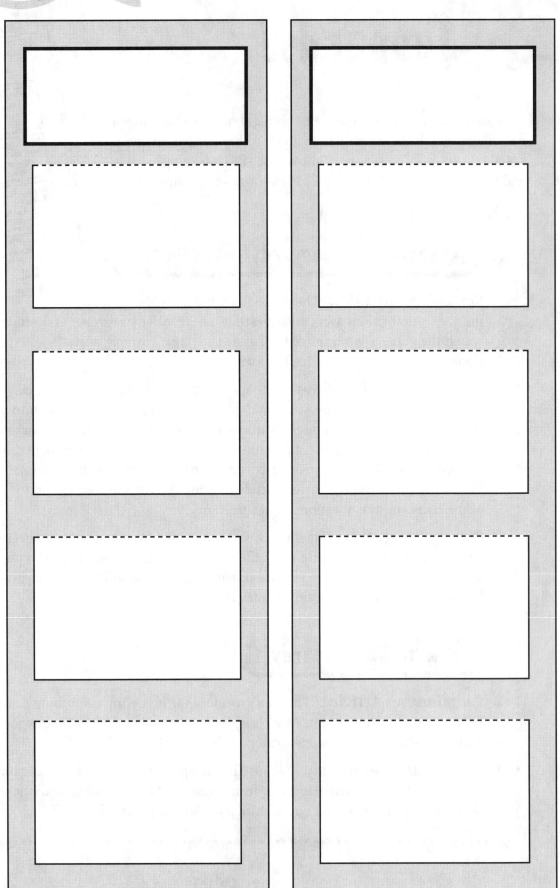

Book Links

BOOK LINKS

Book Title: _____
Author: _____
Student: _____
This book was about: _____   Date Finished: _____
I thought the book was: _____   Parent: _____

Reading is one of the most important subjects students encounter in school. It is required in every subject area and plays an important part in students' futures. While reading skills can be improved through direct teaching, students can learn even more when they simply read for enjoyment. Book links are a quick way for students to respond to books they've read and can be used as part of an incentive program to encourage students to read for pleasure.

Creating the Book Links

* **Using the Template:** Copy the book links template on page 66 on a variety of brightly colored papers. Give each student a sheet of links. Whenever a student finishes reading a book at home, have her fill out the information on the book link, cut it out, get it signed by a parent, and take it to class. Students simply need to write a one-sentence description of the book's plot and a one-sentence response to the book. After students give a short talk about their book, fold their link in half and add it to a chain of book links. When the chain is long enough to reach across the classroom, celebrate by having a popcorn party, or with some other incentive. Stress that this is not a race to see which child can read more books, but rather a group project to celebrate reading.

How to Use Book Links

* **Involving Parents:** Send a letter home to parents informing them of this incentive program and of the importance of reading for pleasure. Ask parents to discuss each book with their child when they sign the book link. Discussing books is one way to foster an excitement for reading.

* **Homework:** As a kick-off for this program, consider not assigning any homework for the first night other than having the students read a book for an assigned period of time. Hopefully students will choose to read for some time each evening.

* **Curriculum-Related Reading:** Reading is important in all subject areas. If you teach a particular subject area, consider linking this program to books related to your curriculum.

* **Displaying the Book Links:** Leave the links up throughout the year so that the class can see how many books they have read.

Book Links Template

Name _____

BOOK LINKS

Book Title: _____
Author: _____
Student: _____
This book was about: _____
I thought the book was: _____

Date Finished: _____
Parent: _____

BOOK LINKS

Book Title: _____
Author: _____
Student: _____
This book was about: _____
I thought the book was: _____

Date Finished: _____
Parent: _____

BOOK LINKS

Book Title: _____
Author: _____
Student: _____
This book was about: _____
I thought the book was: _____

Date Finished: _____
Parent: _____

Story Wheels

In elementary and middle school, students begin to explore the elements of a story: character, setting, problem, solution, and theme. Story wheels are useful devices for reporting on these elements

Creating a Story Wheel

✳ ***Using the Requirement Sheet:*** The requirement sheet on page 68 outlines the basic components of a story wheel. In each section of the wheel, students report on a different element—such as main character, setting, and theme—of a book. You can use the requirement sheet with any novel, making necessary modifications to suit your needs (You may want the students to answer a specific question about the setting, rather than just giving a general description.)

✳ ***Drawing the Circles:*** Large sheets of bulletin-board paper or poster board are perfect for creating story wheels. Students can draw their story wheels by tracing the outline of a large bowl, aluminum tray, or other circular object. They can draw the circle in the center with a compass or by tracing the rim of a glass or jar. Next, they should divide the story wheel into six pie-shaped pieces. After cutting the story wheels out, students can use a ruler and pencil to create the writing lines in each section. They can erase the pencil lines after writing the sentences in pen.

How to Use Story Wheels

✳ ***Relating the Story Wheels to Particular Novels:*** Many novels center around journeys characters take, or they revolve around a theme which features circles or wheels (for example, *The Giver* describes bicycles as a symbol of independence; *Walk Two Moons* centers around the car trip a young girl takes with her grandparents; *Bound for Oregon* describes the journey of a wagon train; *Tuck Everlasting* uses the imagery of wheels throughout the story to reflect the life cycle—ferris wheels, the months on the calendar, the changing of the seasons, and so on). Students can design the story wheels to look like a particular kind of wheel discussed in the story.

Story Wheel Requirement Sheet   Name _____

1 Draw a picture of the main character. Write six vivid adjectives that describe the main character below your picture.

2 Draw a picture of the setting. Describe the setting in a few complete sentences.

3 Draw a picture of the antagonist. List six vivid adjectives that describe this character.

4 Draw a picture of the main problem in the story. Write complete sentences that accurately describe the problem.

5 Draw a picture of the solution to the problem. Write a few complete sentences describing the solution.

6 Write a complete, detailed paragraph that answers the following questions: Why do you think the author wrote this book? What do you think he or she was trying to tell the reader?

Title of Book
Author
Your Name

Make Your Story Wheel 3-D!
You can make the main character or antagonist pop up. Draw the characters on a separate sheet of paper. Draw a background on your story wheel. Cut out the character, add tabs behind it, and glue it to the story wheel.

Comic Strips

The Ugliest Caterpillar by Tina Ladanne

Comics can bring humor and insight to a variety of topics. Because every child is familiar with comics, using them as a reporting device adds an element of fun and makes a report seem less intimidating.

Creating a Comic Strip

* ❋ *Designing the Strip:* Pass out copies of the template on page 70. Students should use this template to draw thumbnail sketches of their comic strips before drawing the final strip on construction paper. (For smaller projects, this template could be used for the final product.) Each panel should contain dialogue—either written by hand or typed and glued in place—and an illustration. Advise students to sketch the illustrations in pencil first before tracing over the pictures with a marker.

* ❋ *The Final Version:* Students can create a large version of their comic strips on an oversize sheet of construction paper. After cutting the paper in half lengthwise, students should tape the two pieces into one long strip. Students can use a ruler and pencil to outline the panels of the comic, leaving a 1-inch margin on the top and 1/4-inch margin on the left, right, and bottom. The width of the panels will vary depending upon the length of the paper and the number of panels required. There should be approximately 1/4 inch between each panel. Students can trace over the panel outlines with black marker and then erase the pencil lines.

How to Use Comic Strips

* ❋ *Historical Comics:* Students can report on a famous historical event in comic strip form. Suggest adding a fanciful element to the strip, such as a talking mouse on the Mayflower or a bird that comments on the Wright Brothers' flight.

* ❋ *Biographies:* Invite students to tell the life story of a famous figure by illustrating the events of his or her life in comic-book form.

* ❋ *The Science Funny Pages:* Students can describe metamorphosis through the eyes of a caterpillar, or create a superhero bee to describe the process of pollination. Comics are only limited by the imagination.

Comic Strip Template

Name ______________________________

Cut along the dotted lines. Glue this tab behind panel 3.

PANEL 3

PANEL 4

PANEL 2

PANEL 5

PANEL 1

PANEL 6

Advertisements

The goal of every advertisement is to grab the viewer's attention and make him or her want to buy, use, join, or switch. Have students use this medium to report on topics they are studying. By designing an ad for a product, they are forced to look at its advantages and highlight these features.

Creating an Advertisement

✳ ***Introduce Selling Techniques:*** Before assigning the project, introduce to students the following techniques advertisers use to entice potential customers:

- **Statistics:** Nine out of ten teachers recommend *35 Ready-to-Go Ways to Publish Students' Research and Writing.*
- **Endorsements:** Jane Smith says, "*35 Ready-to-Go Ways to Publish Students' Research and Writing* is a wonderful resource for teachers of every grade."
- **Join the Bandwagon:** All of the other teachers use *35 Ready-to-Go Ways to Publish Students' Research and Writing* to improve their teaching methods.
- **Exaggeration:** *35 Ready-to Go-Ways to Publish Students' Research and Writing* is the best professional book for teachers ever written.
- **Implication:** If you use *35 Ready-to-Go Ways to Publish Students' Research and Writing*, your students will enjoy school more and improve their grades.

After discussing these techniques, pass out old magazines, newspapers and advertising circulars. Have students work in pairs looking for examples of each of these techniques. Discuss the findings with the class.

✳ ***Designing the Ads:*** Pass out large sheets of white construction paper for students to use for their ads. Students can draw and color the ads, or use clippings from magazine ads. Specify the written requirements to students; for example, whether or not you want a complete paragraph in explanatory text, if the ad needs a slogan, etc.

How to Use Advertisements

✳ ***Cross-Curricular Advertising:*** Students can create advertisements to persuade people to read a book, to recruit soldiers for the Civil War, to advertise a new (or old) invention, to prevent pollution, or to attract people to their state. Adapt this activity to any number of subject areas.

Roll Movies

In the business world, companies present slide shows to accompany and accent their corporate reports. Roll movies, too, make great presentation tools. Students can use them as a visual aid when giving an oral report. Teachers can use them to capture students' attention by presenting a lesson in a unique way.

Creating a Roll Movie

* **Materials:** To make a roll movie, each student will need a ruler, scissors, tape, markers, a box, and two wooden dowels. (The dowels should be about 6 inches longer than the width of the box.) Provide the class with a roll of white bulletin-board or craft paper.

* **Making the Roll Movie Box:** Each student will need an empty box to make a roll movie. To get started, students will need to prepare their boxes.
    1. Have each student draw a window on the front of the box and cut the window out. The window should be approximately 3 inches from the sides of the box.
    2. Students should cut a hole on each side of the box about 1 inch above the window. Then they should cut another hole on each side about inch below the window. The holes need to be large enough for the dowel to fit through.
    3. Students should push the dowels through the holes so the ends protrude from the sides of the box.

* **Making the Roll Movie:**
    1. Have students cut long strips of white paper from the roll of paper to use for their movies. The strip of paper should be approximately 2 inches wider than the width of the window in their boxes.
    2. Students should use colored markers to create the panels of the roll movie. The first panel should start about 8 inches from the top of paper to allow the top to be rolled around the top dowel. The pictures should be as large as the window in the box and should be drawn vertically, one on top of the other, because that is how they will be seen as they scroll up the window. Students should skip a few inches between each of the panels. Remind students not to put important information near the sides because an inch on each side will be hidden behind the sides of the window.

✳ ***Putting It All Together:*** To complete their roll movies, students should tape the top of the strip to the top dowel, with the panels showing through the window. Turn the dowel so the paper rolls around the top dowel. Tape the end of the last panel to the bottom dowel. Students rewind the movie and it's ready to be shown.

How to Use Roll Movies

✳ ***Unique Picture Books:*** Some picture books are useful for teaching certain concepts to students. For example, *The True Story of the Three Little Pigs* by John Scieska lends itself to a lesson about point of view. However, by the time students get to the upper grades they've probably heard or read these stories several times. Drawing or copying some of the pictures from the picture book and presenting the story as a roll movie makes the story fresh again for the students.

✳ ***Shoe-Box Reports:*** Shoe boxes can be used for mini-roll movies. Students can present book reports using this medium, and then the movies can be lined up on a shelf or table. "Shoe Box Biographies" can present the lives of famous people. Consider having the students draw a square at the bottom of each frame in which they write captions to accompany the illustrations.

Newscasts and Radio Reports

Nothing sparks students' imaginations more than creative dramatics. Writing a play and performing it infuses the learning environment with excitement. However, mounting a full-scale production is often too time-consuming for most classrooms. Creating newscasts and radio reports accomplishes the same goals, yet are more manageable undertakings.

Creating Newscasts and Radio Reports

* **Using a Video Camera:** Brainstorm the elements of a nightly news program with your students. Assign a topic for students to turn into a newscast, either as a whole-class activity or in small groups. Invite them to use visual aids such as costumes, charts, and props to make the newscast as realistic as possible. Videotape students' finished newscasts. The students will love watching themselves on TV.

* **Using a Tape Recorder:** Assign topics for students to turn into radio reports and tape-record them. Students can use sound effects to create the illusion of on-site reporting, giving it a "you are there" feel. Add the tapes to your listening center for the students to listen to throughout the year.

How to Use Newscasts and Radio Reports

* **Historical Newscasts:** Students can write a newscast or radio report as if it took place during a historic period or event. Using the Revolutionary War as an example, they could include newsworthy events (the Boston Tea Party), weather, (the snowstorm at Valley Forge), politics (writing the Declaration of Independence), sports (lawn bowling), and entertainment (Restoration comedies).

* **Talk Shows:** Students can write a talk show where historical figures or characters from a novel confront each other to work out their issues.

* **Dramatic Serials:** Go to your local library and find a tape of an old radio serial. After listening to it with the class, challenge students to write and perform their own radio plays. They might use a favorite short story or novel for inspiration. Encourage them to create sound effects for added atmosphere.

* **Comparing the Decades:** Divide the class into small groups. Each group can research and report on a different decade from the 20th century. They can dress in the styles of the decade as they present a newscast of major events and cultural activities from those years.

Math Logs

Learning mathematical formulas, terminology, and concepts is like learning a foreign language to many students. Having them create and update a log of mathematical information throughout the year is an excellent way to ensure that students have the information at their fingertips. To encourage students to keep their logs current and record information carefully, allow them to occasionally use their math logs during tests.

Creating a Math Log

* **Using the Template:** You can use the quicksheet templates on page 61 for math logs. Makes copies of the template and hand out to students. As students complete an entry on a quicksheet, they can cut it out and punch two holes in the top of the paper. Students can fasten all their entries together with metal binder rings. To make their math logs more durable, students can make front and back covers from cardboard.

* **Number the Pages:** At the top of each entry, students should write the page number from the textbook where the term or formula can be found. This will help them find the information in case they need to review it in more depth.

How to Use Math Logs

* **Terms:** Whenever students come across an unfamiliar math term, such as integer, percent, or negative number, they should write the term at the top of the page, draw an illustration of the term, and define it.

* **Formulas:** Students should include any formulas they learn, such as converting fractions to decimals, in their math logs. Students can write the name of the formula at the top of the page, describe how it works, and write an example.

* **Journal Entries:** It is often helpful for students to write a description of how to solve a problem in paragraph form. This helps them think linguistically about math. They should use words like first, next, then, and finally when describing the steps of problem solving.

Wanted Posters

Wanted posters evoke images of lawless individuals, of people who cause problems for other people. In other words… antagonists. Students learn about antagonists when reading novels, when studying history, and when reporting on current events. Having students create a wanted poster of the antagonist can help you evaluate their understanding of who the antagonist is and what the antagonist did.

Creating a Wanted Poster

✳ *Using the Template:* Pass out a copy of the template on page 77 to each student. Have students draw a colorful, detailed picture of the antagonist in the box and write a complete paragraph describing who the antagonist is, what he or she did, and what he or she is wanted for.

How to Use Wanted Posters

✳ *Book Reports:* Have students create a wanted poster for a story's villain or antagonist. This gives them another way of exploring a book.

✳ *Historical Reports:* Students can create wanted posters of infamous people from history or today. They can relate to a time period or event the class is studying.

✳ *Grammar's Most Wanted:* Students can create posters that feature grammatical mistakes. They can write a grammatically incorrect sentence in the box using creative lettering and explain the grammatical rule on the lines below it. (For example, "Don't use no double negatives." "Be sure, you use commas in the right place." "About those fragments." "Sit this plate on the table.")

Display Idea

✳ *Most Wanted:* Hang the wanted posters on a bulletin board under the title ROOM 201'S MOST WANTED or ANTAGONISTS FROM THE PAST.

Wanted Poster Template

Draw a detailed picture of the antagonist in the box and write a complete paragraph describing the antagonist.

WANTED

_____
_____
_____
_____
_____
_____
_____
_____

Class Quilts

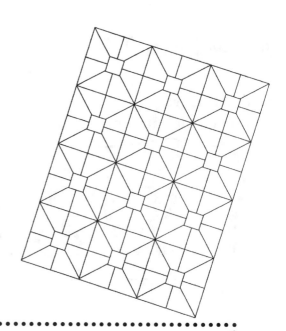

Every class has a unique personality, a personality which is colored by the individuals who make up the class and by the way they interact with one another. Class quilts can be assembled to show how each member of the class is part of the whole.

Creating a Class Quilt

✳ **Taking the Pictures:** Take a Polaroid snapshot of each student. (You can also use a regular camera, but you will have to get the pictures developed.) The students' heads should be about 1 1/2 inches tall in the final snapshot. An alternative is to have students bring in a wallet-size copy of their school pictures.

✳ **Using the Template:** Pass out of a copy of the template on page 79 to each student. Have students follow the directions on the template to create their section of the class quilt. Tell students to consider making their designs in repetitive patterns. For example, if their favorite sport is football, they can create a repetitive pattern of footballs. This makes the quilt squares look more like strips of material.

✳ **Assembling the Quilt** After students finish their panels and cut them out, have them lay the panels next to each other, face down. Tape the panels together into one large quilt. Hang the quilt on the wall or bulletin board.

How to Use Class Quilts

✳ **"ME" Quilts:** Following the directions on the template students create a quilt panel about themselves. This is a great beginning-of-the-year exercise to help instill a sense of community in the classroom—every individual is a part of the whole.

✳ **Novel Quilts:** Students draw a picture of the main character in the center box and design a quilt pattern related to that character.

✳ **Historical Quilts:** Students draw a picture of a famous historical figure in the center box and draw pictures of events, accomplishments, people, places, and things related to that person.

Class Quilt Template

Name _____

- Cut out your picture and glue it in the center of the box below.
- In each section, create designs and draw pictures describing things about you: goals you have in life; family members; your favorite movie, song, school subject, sport, food, hobby, pet, etc.
- Use your imagination. Fill the entire panel with color.
- In one of the sections write your name in fancy lettering.
- Cut the panel out and give it to your teacher.

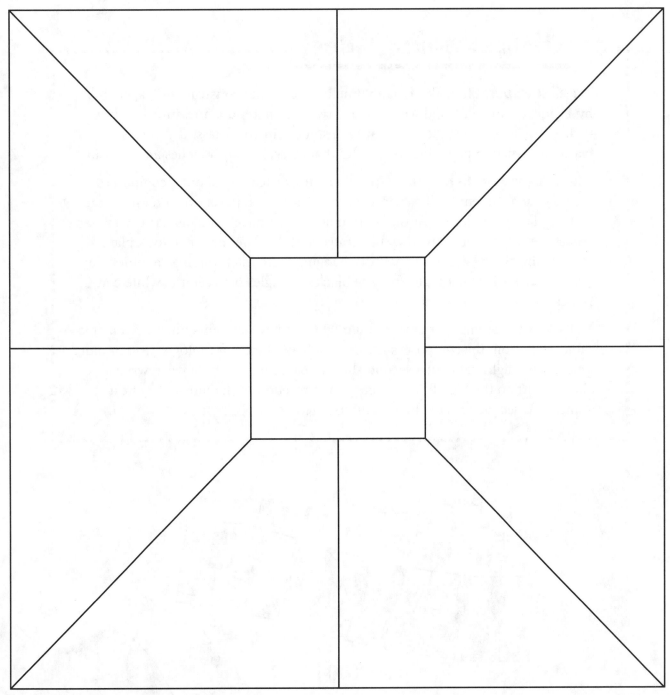

Musical Timelines

Students are often exposed to the lives and works of famous composers in music class, at concerts or assemblies, or when studying biographies of famous people. Creating a musical timeline based on the life of the composer lays the musician's life out in a visual display and teaches students about sequencing events.

Creating a Musical Timeline

* ***Pre-Cut Paper:*** To make a piano timeline, cut white construction paper (8 ½ by 11 inches) in half lengthwise to make two rectangles that measure 4 ¼ by 11 inches. You'll need one rectangle for each student in your class. Cut sheets of black construction paper into rectangles that measure 2 by 5 inches and set aside.

* ***Illustrating and Reporting:*** After studying or reading about a composer's life, ask each student to illustrate a scene from the composer's life on one of the rectangular "piano keys". At the bottom of the key, have students write a few sentences describing the scene they illustrated and the date the scene took place. Display the piano keys in the hallway, hanging them in chronological order. To complete your keyboard, glue or tape black rectangles between the white construction-paper piano keys.

* ***Variations*** For younger grades you might just have students illustrate a memorable event from the composer's life but not hang them chronologically. For older grades you might pass out a second sheet of paper in which they can write a short report on the life of the composer or a reaction to the music they heard. Attach this second sheet behind the illustrated keys.